STRANGE CREATURES

by SEYMOUR SIMON
illustrated by PAMELA CARROLL

FOUR WINDS PRESS
NEW YORK

LIBRARY OF CONGRESS CATALOGING IN PUBLICATION DATA

Simon, Seymour.
Strange creatures.

Summary: Describes a number of animals that look or behave oddly or have strange powers or abilities, including the hoatzin, tuatara, grunion, and gecko.
1. Animals—Miscellanea—Juvenile literature.
[1. Animals—Miscellanea] I. Carroll, Pamela. II. Title.
QL49.S5193   591   81-4433
ISBN 0-590-07745-7   AACR2

PUBLISHED BY FOUR WINDS PRESS
A DIVISION OF SCHOLASTIC INC., NEW YORK, N.Y.
TEXT COPYRIGHT © 1981 BY SEYMOUR SIMON
ILLUSTRATIONS COPYRIGHT © 1981 BY PAMELA CARROLL
ALL RIGHTS RESERVED
PRINTED IN THE UNITED STATES OF AMERICA
LIBRARY OF CONGRESS CATALOG CARD NUMBER: 81-4433
BOOK DESIGN BY LUCY MARTIN BITZER
1   2   3   4   5   85   84   83   82   81

INTRODUCTION

SOME TINY BIRDS BUILD NESTS THAT ARE as big as haystacks. One kind of fish can live enclosed in a block of mud without food or water for as long as four years. There are small mammals that eat their own weight in food every three hours. Without food, they would starve to death in a day. There are over one million different kinds of animals living on the earth today. Some of these, such as dogs and cats, you may see every day. Others you may see in zoos or on farms. But many others are not familiar to most people. This book is about some of the strange animals that live all over the world. In this book you will find animals that look strange (at least to our eyes), that behave in odd ways, that have strange powers or abilities. Sometimes, scientists know how an animal's strange appearance or behavior helps it to survive. But other times, scientists cannot explain the reasons for an animal's looks or the way it acts. No one book can cover all the strange animals of the world. But this book tells you about some of the very strangest.

A Real Vampire

NOT ALL VAMPIRES ARE MYTHS LIKE Count Dracula. Some vampires are only too real. The vampire bat lives from Mexico south into Central and South America. It lives only on blood. The vampire bat is not a very scary-looking animal. Like all bats, the vampire is a mammal. Its body is covered with short gray or brown hair. Its body is just about three inches long, and it has a wingspread of about one foot. The bat has razor-sharp front teeth. It uses its teeth to make a slit in the skin of its victim. Then it laps up the blood that comes out of the wound. The cut is made so skillfully that the victim may not even wake up from its sleep. Vampire bats attack their victims only at night. The bats often feed on cattle, horses, and other domestic animals. Less often, vampire bats will also attack people. While the wound heals quickly, repeated feedings on the same animal can make it weak and ill. Even more serious are the diseases that can be passed on by the bat. Among the worst of the diseases is rabies, which often results in the death of the victim. Vampire bats live in colonies of about one dozen or more animals. During the daylight hours, the bats roost in cracks and crevices in the walls of caves. If disturbed, the bats can run along the walls with surprising speed. When its wings are folded, the bat walks like a four-footed animal, or hops like a frog.

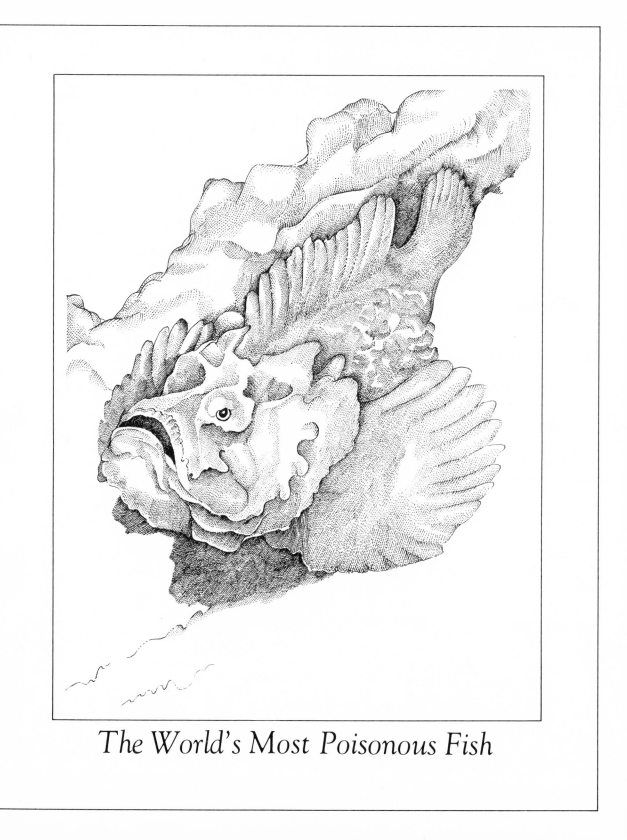

The World's Most Poisonous Fish

THE STONEFISH GETS ITS NAME BECAUSE it looks just like a stone or rock. When a stonefish rests on the sea bottom, it is almost invisible. Any small animal that comes near is quickly swallowed. But even if a large animal comes near, a stonefish does not move away. This makes it possible for a person to step upon one accidentally. And stepping on a stonefish can be a very nasty experience. Along a stonefish's back are thirteen large spines. The spines will shoot a deadly poison into anyone stepping on them. The pain is immediate and terrible and it lasts for hours before it gradually lessens. There are stories of people who tried to cut off their own legs, so great was their agony. A person who has received a large amount of the poison usually dies within six hours. And even small amounts can lead to the loss of a toe or a foot. If a person does recover from the poison it may take as long as six months to get over the attack. There is no doubt that the stonefishes are the most poisonous fishes in the world. Fortunately, they are not very common. They are found in the shallow ocean waters around Australia, some Pacific islands, and part of the Indian Ocean. Similar fish are found in other tropical seas.

The Flying Dragons

THERE ARE ABOUT THREE DOZEN RElated kinds of lizards called flying dragons that live in Southeast Asia. They all have loose folds of skin between their front and hind legs. The skin is supported by ribs along both sides of their bodies. When these slender, eight- to ten-inch lizards rest or climb about a branch, the skin and ribs are folded back out of the way. But when the lizards leap to a distant tree, the ribs and skin open up like a pair of wings. The lizards can glide for sixty feet through the air before they come in for a landing on a tree trunk. They always land with their heads upward. The lizards spend most of their lives off the ground in the trees. They eat all kinds of spiders, insects, and other small animals. After they eat all the food they can find on one tree, they launch themselves into the air toward a nearby tree to look for more prey. The only time the flying dragons come to the ground is to lay their eggs. The body of the flying dragon is a kind of drab gray or brown that blends in with the tree bark. But the wings are brilliantly colored, bright orange or yellow with black stripes. They also have a long pouch beneath their throats and a flap on each side of their head. You can easily see how they get their name.

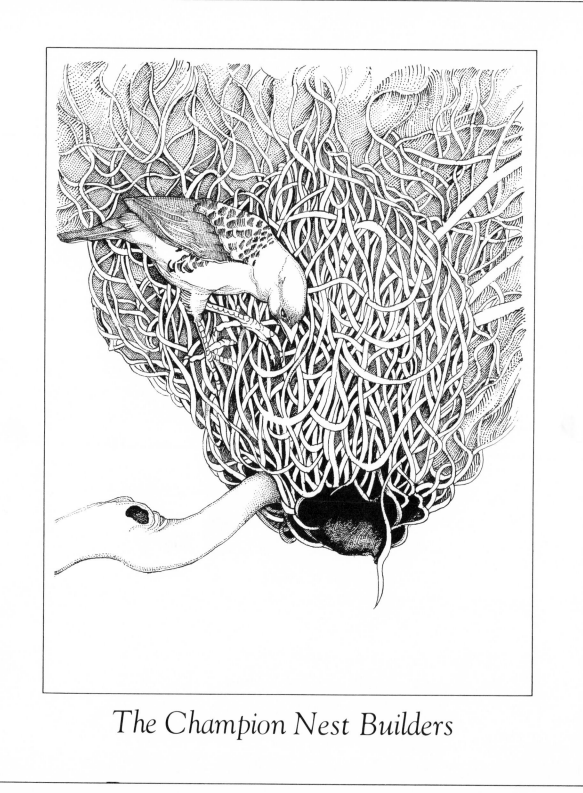

The Champion Nest Builders

THE SOCIAL WEAVERBIRD IS A CLOSE relative of the common house sparrow. But whereas the sparrow makes a small, untidy nest on a window ledge or on a tree branch, the weaverbird makes a huge "apartment house" of a nest. The social weavers live on the dry, flat lands of southern Africa. They live in large colonies of thirty or more pairs of birds. The birds work together in building their huge nests. But each pair of weavers has it own "apartment," or nesting chamber. The nests are huge masses of straw and grass. They are often located among the thorny branches of an acacia tree. The nests may be ten or fifteen feet high and six to ten feet wide. Some nests have been known to house more than one hundred weaver families. There are many other kinds of weavers that build unusual nests. And while none are as large as the nests of the social weavers, some are quite interesting. Some kinds of tropical weavers build nests that look like wine flasks. The nests hang down from tree branches or tall grasses. The male weavers usually do most of the nest building. Most kinds of weaverbirds are excellent nest builders, but there are a few exceptions. Widowbirds, members of the weaver family, do not build nests at all. Instead, the females lay their eggs in the nests of other birds. The host birds seem not to spot the difference. They hatch out the widowbird's eggs and then raise the young.

The Fish That Lives Without Food or Water

THE AFRICAN LUNGFISH CAN LIVE WITH-out food or water for as long as four years! Lungfish live in swampy places, streams, and lakes. These places may dry up during regular dry seasons or during times of drought. When this happens, the lungfish sink into the mud at the bottom. As long as the mud remains soft, the lungfish just swims up and takes a breath of air every twenty minutes or so. But when the mud begins to harden, the lungfish prepares itself for its long summer rest, called "estivation." It folds its six-foot-long body into a U shape, head and tail facing upward. Its skin makes a thin mucus covering that protects the lungfish from drying out. The mud bakes hard in the sun and finally the fish is completely enclosed. Changes now take place in the lungfish's body, allowing it to live at a very slow rate. It is a state of deep sleep called estivation—a kind of hibernation during hot seasons. The lungfish remains in its stonelike protection until the rains come and soften the mud.

A Tiny Killer

THE SHREWS ARE AMONG THE SMALLEST of all the mammals. Many shrews weigh about as much as a dime and are about the size of a small mouse. Even the largest shrew is only about as big as a rat. Yet ounce for ounce, no more deadly creature exists. Shrews are almost constantly on the hunt for food. They can eat their own weight in food *every three hours.* Without food, a shrew will starve to death in a day. Shrews feed on insects, earthworms, and other small animals without backbones. Some shrews will also attack and eat mice, small frogs, salamanders, and even other shrews. A hungry shrew will attack an animal twice or more its own size. A shrew seems to live at double speed. Its tiny heart beats a thousand times a minute. It may die of old age when it is only one year old. A shrew can be killed by any sudden loud noise. Shrews are almost impossible to keep for long in captivity. The American short-tailed shrew is common in the eastern United States. It lives beneath the leaves in fields and forests. It is so small and quick that it is rarely seen. But this little one-ounce killer has a poison similar to the venom of a cobra. A drop of its saliva injected into a mouse will quickly cause its death. Because of their small size, shrews are of little or no danger to people. In fact, shrews are a great help to farmers because they kill so many insects and rodent pests.

A Bird That Smells Bad

THE HOATZIN OF SOUTH AMERICA GIVES off a peculiar odor. In fact, the local people call it the stinking pheasant. But that's not the only strange feature of the hoatzin. It has eyelashes—a great rarity among birds. And young hoatzins have claws on their wings as well as on their feet. The hoatzin lives in the forests surrounding tropical rivers. The birds cannot fly very well: They thrash about as they move from branch to branch. On the ground, they hop about from place to place. The hoatzin is about the size of a small chicken. It builds a crude nest of sticks in a low bush or tree. The young are featherless. They climb all over the tree with the aid of the claws on their wings. And that's not all. When the chick falls into the water, as it often does, it can dive and swim without difficulty. It then returns to its nest by crawling up the tree trunk just like a little lizard. In some ways, a newborn hoatzin reminds you more of a prehistoric reptile than of a modern-day bird. A few weeks after hatching, the claws disappear from the wings and feathers grow. An adult hoatzin looks more birdlike. It has a small head with a feathery comb and a long feathered tail.

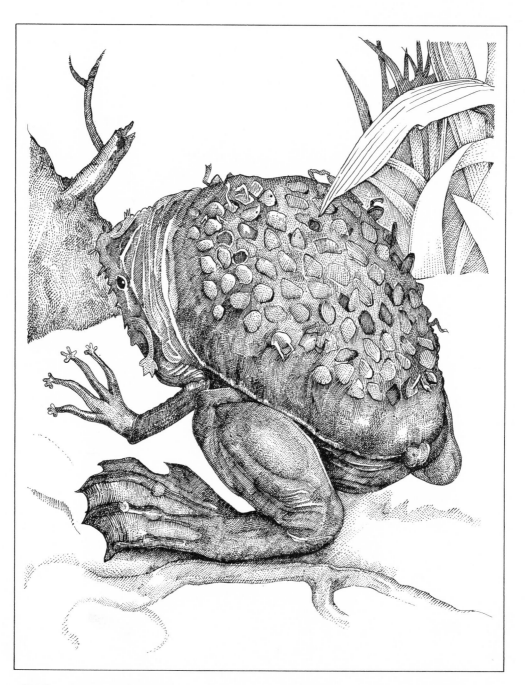

The Toad That Carries Eggs on Its Back

THE FEMALE SURINAM TOAD CARES FOR its eggs in one of the strangest imaginable ways. As the female lays eggs, the male fertilizes them and presses them one by one into the soft skin on the female's back. At first, the eggs just stick to the skin. But after a while, each egg sinks into a little pocket that forms to receive it. Then a covering of skin grows over the pocket. The young toads hatch and develop, each in its own little compartment. Some weeks later, the female rubs the thick skin off her back and the young are set free. Each young toad looks like a tiny version of its parents. The Surinam toad looks very odd. Its body is flat and square and its head is flat and triangular. Its snout looks as if it had been cut off. There are bits of flesh at the ends of its mouth which serve as fish lures. And each of its long fingers has a four-pointed, starlike tip. The toad rarely leaves the muddy streams in South America where it lives. It sits on the bottom with its long fingers spread out on either side of its mouth. When a small animal touches the fingers, the toad opens its wide mouth and swallows its prey whole. The Surinam toad does not have a tongue. This is unusual; most toads and frogs have tongues they use to catch insects in the air. But as a tongue is useless in the water, the Surinam toad is not handi-capped by being without one.

19

A Living Fossil

THE TUATARA IS THE ONLY LIVING MEMber of an ancient group of reptiles that lived nearly two hundred million years ago. All of the others of its kind died many millions of years ago. But the tuatara still survives on some of the islands off the coast of New Zealand. The tuatara actually has three eyes. The third eye lies in the middle of its head and is covered by a transparent scale. In young tuataras, the eye can detect light from dark. But as the tuatara grows older, the eye becomes overgrown by skin and is not used. The two-foot-long lizard has a row of spines that reach from its neck down the middle of its back and tail. The tuatara lives in a burrow by day. During the night it comes out to feed on insects and other small animals. The female tuatara lays her eggs in a hollow dug in the ground. The eggs are buried beneath the soil where they remain for as long as a year. The young finally are ready to hatch and break through the tough skin of the eggs. Then the four- to five-inch young dig their way to the surface. They grow slowly and may live for more than twenty years. Not many years ago, the tuatara lived on the mainland of New Zealand. But European settlers and the animals they brought soon killed off the ancient lizard. The tuatara is now legally protected and cannot be hunted or otherwise disturbed.

The Fish on a Timetable

OFF THE COAST OF SOUTHERN CALIFORnia, live silvery little fish called grunion. Every two weeks throughout the spring, millions of grunion ride in to shore on the highest tides of the full and new moon. The grunion swim high up on the sandy beaches with the waves. As the waters roll back to the sea, the fish are left stranded on the sand. The beach is covered with thousands upon thousands of wriggling fish. Each female grunion digs herself into the sand, tail first, until she is more than half buried. Then she lays about two thousand eggs underground. The male grunion curve around on top of the sand. The milt (sperm) of the males sifts through the sand to fertilize the eggs. In less than a minute the spawning is over. The grunion wriggle back toward the sea. Finally, they catch a wave which carries them back to deeper water. The eggs do not hatch until the next high tide comes in two weeks. Two or three minutes after they have been freed by the high tide, the eggs hatch. The baby grunion are carried out to sea by the retreating waters. The timing is always exactly right. The eggs are always laid at the highest tides. They will not hatch until they are uncovered by the next high tide. When the young hatch, they are about one-quarter inch long and able to swim immediately.

A Long-Distance Traveler

THE ARCTIC TERN MAKES THE LONGEST regular journeys of any known animal—twenty-two thousand miles, from the Arctic to the Antarctic and back. Each migration takes two months. These birds spend the summer months in their breeding grounds above the Arctic Circle. Here they lay their eggs and raise their young during the long weeks of continuous daylight. But when the sun dips below the horizon and fall comes, these small relatives of gulls leave their nesting grounds. The first part of their long migration takes them across the North Atlantic to the coast of Europe. During their travels over the ocean, the terns do not stop to rest. After a few weeks of feeding along European shores, the terns are on the move again. They fly along the coasts of Africa until they reach the cold, food-rich waters of the Antarctic. It is summer now in the Antarctic (it is winter in the Arctic). The birds dive for small fish in the long daylight hours. The waters teem with fish and the terns build up their body strength. When fall comes to the Antarctic, the terns start their return journey to their breeding grounds in the far north.

The Slowest Mammal

THE TREE SLOTH NEVER GOES ANYWHERE in a hurry. In fact, it almost never goes *anywhere!* **T**he sloth spends most of its life hanging upside down from the branches of trees. It holds on to the branches with its long, hooked claws. It is almost impossible to pull a sloth off a branch. Even in death, it will continue to hold on.   **T**he three-toed sloth may spend its entire life in one tree. It slowly picks and munches the leaves and fruit of the tree. After it eats everything within reach, it slowly moves hand over hand to a new feeding place.   **T**he sloth's long, coarse hair hangs down from its back. During the rainy season, its hair often turns greenish because of the growth of algae. Then the sloth looks like a mossy tree branch.   **T**he sloth even sleeps hanging on to a branch in an upside-down position. It keeps hold with all four feet, while its head hangs down between its front legs. Each day, a sloth spends about eighteen hours sleeping. But it still seems tired when it awakens.   **S**trangely, the sloth is a better swimmer than a walker. In the South American forests where it lives, a sloth may sometimes swim across a wide lake. Perhaps when it gets across, the sloth has to rest for a few years to get back its energy!

The Animal That Changes Color

THERE ARE MORE THAN EIGHTY DIFFERent kinds of chameleons. Most of them are found in central and southern Africa. The animals called "chameleons" found in the United States are really anoles, a different kind of lizard. All chameleons can change the color of their skins. They can change from green or yellow to dark gray and they can even show spots or lines. This helps them to match their backgrounds. But chameleons rarely get a perfect blend of every color. The chameleons can change colors because of different color cells in their skins. Some of the cells are yellow, others are whitish, while still others are black. The cells can grow larger or smaller in a short time. As the cells change in size, the lizard's skin seems to change in color. Chameleons are remarkable in other ways as well. A chameleon's tongue has a sticky tip, just right for catching insects. The chameleon can shoot out its tongue with lightning speed when an insect is more than a foot away. Many chameleons have tongues that are longer than their body and tail combined! The chameleon's eyes are housed in little bumps on each side of its head. The two eyes can look in different directions. For example, one eye can look upward while the other eye is looking backward. When the chameleon spots an insect, however, both eyes focus on its prey.

A Fish That Fishes for Food

THE GOOSEFISH USES ONE OF ITS SPINES as a fishing rod complete with bait. The spine is located just behind the upper lip. It has a leaflike flap of skin at the tip. This is jerked back and forth over the mouth like a lure. Any small fish attracted by the lure is swallowed in one gulp. The goosefish appears to be almost all head. And the head looks like it is almost all mouth. The mouth of the goosefish is so large, in fact, that it can swallow fish almost as large as itself. A large goosefish can reach a length of three or four feet. This enormous mouth is pointed upward. The lower jaw sticks out far beyond the upper. Many sharp, fanglike teeth line both jaws. The teeth may be up to one inch long. They are back-curved so that they keep prey from slipping out. The Atlantic coast goosefish has an enormous appetite to go along with its big mouth. It eats all kinds of fishes and other sea animals. It will also eat ducks and geese—a food that gave the fish its name—which may be swimming on the surface. One goosefish's stomach contained seventy-five herrings. Another contained twenty flounders. A third held seven ducks! Sometimes the food in a goosefish's stomach weighs half as much as the whole fish—twenty pounds or more. Sometimes a goosefish will try to swallow too large an animal and it will choke to death.

The Lizard That Can Walk on the Ceiling

A GECKO CAN WALK ACROSS A CEILING as easily as you walk across the floor. No, it doesn't have suction pads on its feet. Instead, each of the gecko's toes has thousands of tiny hooks that catch on to almost any surface. Geckos make up a large family of lizards. Some kinds of geckos live in underground burrows. Other kinds live in trees or in buildings. Geckos are found mostly in Asia and Africa, although some are found in the Americas as well. Most geckos are small, insect-eating lizards that are active during the night. Nearly all the geckos have a voice of some kind—a squeak, a cluck, a chirp, a croak, or a screech. Some geckos make a deafening racket when a number of them sound off at once. The word *gecko* itself comes from the sound made by one of the family members. Geckos have eyes which are exactly suited for night vision. They have very large pupils which let in any light that is available. In addition, some geckos have eye pupils which have bumps or lobes. These result in a much brighter and sharper image than a single round pupil could provide.

The Champion Egg Layer

THERE ARE ONLY A FEW KINDS OF BIRDS that lay eggs larger than the eggs of the New Zealand kiwi. But no other bird or other animal even comes close to the kiwi when you compare the size of the egg to the size of the animal. The kiwi weighs about four pounds, and a kiwi egg weighs about one pound! It takes about seventy-five or eighty days for a kiwi egg to hatch—almost another record. The male kiwi sits on the egg during that time. When a kiwi chick is born, it is fully feathered. But it still takes three or four years for the chick to grow into an adult. The kiwi is a bird that cannot fly. When a kiwi runs about, it wobbles from side to side like a child taking its first steps. About the size of a large farm chicken, the kiwi is covered with long, hairlike feathers. Its wings are only about two inches long, and it has very small eyes. The kiwi gets its name from the peculiar sound it makes during courtship—a whistling noise that sounds like *kee-wee*. The kiwi bird has a long, curved bill that is unlike those of most other birds. There are nostrils at the tip of the bill, and the kiwi has a good sense of smell. The kiwi uses its bill as a probe looking for earthworms, grubs, and insects in the soil.

A Mammal That Lays an Egg

THE SPINY ANTEATER, OR ECHIDNA, IS an egg-laying mammal that lives in Australia, Tasmania, and New Guinea. The echidna egg has a thin, leathery shell and a large yolk like that of a reptile egg. Usually the female lays only a single egg in a year. But she does not hatch the egg the way a reptile or a bird does. She places the egg in a pouch on her abdomen, something like a kangaroo's pouch. The egg hatches in a few days in this built-in incubator. The young echidna does not have to leave the pouch in order to eat. It laps up milk that comes directly from the mammary glands inside the pouch. The young echidna stays and grows in the pouch until its spines become a nuisance to its mother. An adult echidna is about twenty inches long. Its body is covered with sharp spines and coarse hair. Its mouth is long and beaklike, much like that of a bird. It has powerful claws and digs into the ground with great speed. Males have a poisonous spine on their hind legs. Oddly, the echidna has no teeth. Its main foods are termites and ants.
It will slash through an ant nest with its claws, and then
stick its beak into the earth searching for insects.
Its long tongue snatches up the ants and then
crushes them inside its mouth.

A Shocking Fish

THE ELECTRIC EEL CAN DELIVER FOUR hundred volts of electricity at one ampere. That makes it the most powerful and dangerous electric fish in the world. This South American river fish can knock down and stun a horse in the water at a distance of twenty feet. It can even kill a person who touches it. There are also records of people who have drowned after being knocked unconscious by an electric eel. A full-grown electric eel may be as much as eight feet long. Half of its body weight is made up of the special muscles that produce electricity. The electric eel can keep up the discharges for days at a time. Electric eels use their electricity to get food as well as to protect themselves. They swallow whole the small fishes, frogs, and other animals stunned by their discharges. Still another use of the discharge is for navigation. The eel gives off a regular series of mild charges. These are used as a kind of radar to help the fish find its way about. The electric eel is not really an eel. Its long body and lack of some fins make it look eellike, but it is not related to the true eels.

An Animal in Armor

THE ARMADILLO LOOKS LIKE IT IS dressed in armor. Its body is covered with a bony shell. The shell is made up of bony plates and covered with horny scales. The middle of the shell is flexible and acts like a hinge so that the armadillo can bend fairly easily. It can even curl up and protect its soft underparts. The armadillo's head is also covered by an armored plate. And some armadillos even have their tails enclosed in armor. You might think that with all its armor an armadillo is ready for a life of warfare. But that is not at all the case. The armadillo is a very peaceful animal. It cannot even bite; its teeth are all in the back of its mouth, not up front. When threatened by an enemy, armadillos hurry off in the opposite direction. Moving as fast as their short legs can carry them, they try to reach the burrows in which they live. Their armor protects them from enemies as well as the sharp spines of cactus plants that they trample in their rush to retreat. The nine-banded armadillo is found in Central America and Mexico, and from Texas to Florida. This three-foot-long mammal is sometimes hunted for food. In many places it is called the poor man's pig. The giant armadillo that lives in Brazil may measure more than four feet long and weigh well over one hundred pounds. Mostly, armadillos eat termites and other insects.

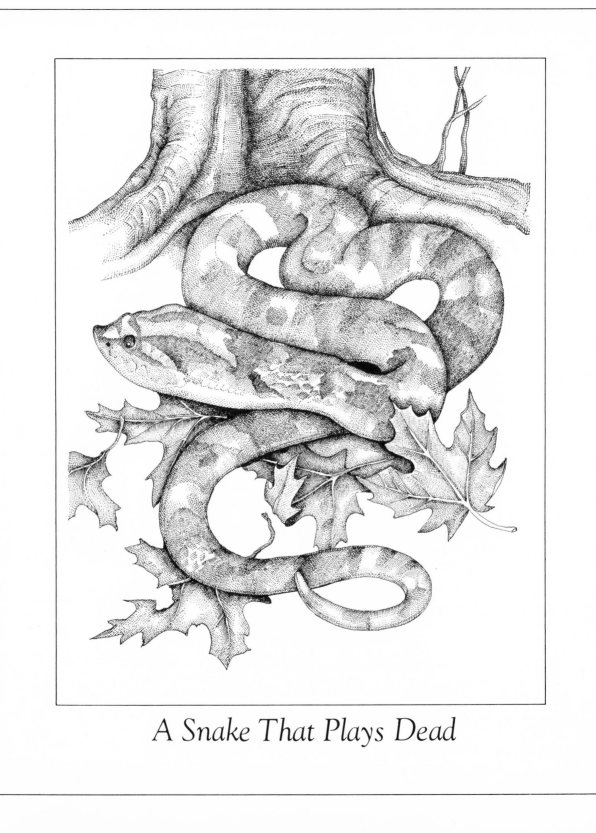

A Snake That Plays Dead

THE EASTERN HOGNOSE SNAKE IS A common nonpoisonous snake found along the East Coast of the United States. It is a thick-bodied, slow-moving snake with a wide head. Its average length is about two to three feet. If you come upon a hognose snake in the field, it puts on quite an act. Instead of gliding away quietly as most snakes would do, the hognose holds its ground. It flattens and coils its body. It hisses loudly and rises part way off the ground. It moves back and forth as if getting ready to strike. Its actions are enough to scare off most intruders. But instead of running away, suppose you just stand your ground. Then the hognose goes into the second part of its act. It twists its body as if in agony. Then it rolls over on its back and lies perfectly still. Its mouth is open and its tongue lies limply on the ground. The hognose looks as if it has just died a horrible death. You can pick up the hognose and carry it around, and it will remain limp and lifeless. But if you place it back on the ground right-side up, it promptly rolls over on its belly and continues its death act! Interestingly, the hognose will never bite a person, even when angry. Even if it strikes, its mouth is closed. It depends upon good acting to be left alone. The hognose's act must be somewhat successful because its local names include puff adder, sand viper, and spreadhead—names usually given to dangerous, poisonous snakes.

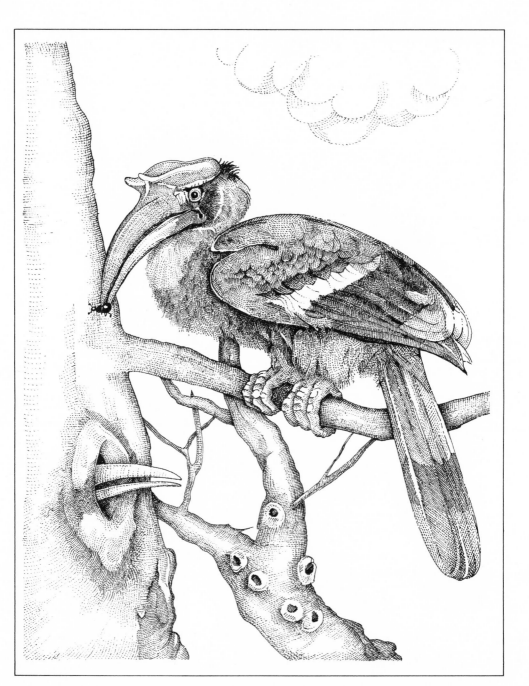

A Bird That Imprisons Itself

ORNBILLS ARE LARGE BIRDS THAT LIVE in the tropical forests of Asia and Africa. They are named for their very large, curved bills. The top of the bill has a bright-colored, horny growth called a casque. The nesting habits of hornbills are among the strangest in all the animal world. After mating, the female hornbill goes inside a hollow tree to lay her eggs. Then she begins to seal herself into the tree with a layer of mud. With most kinds of hornbills, the male helps from outside. He gathers mud from the forest floor and passes mud pellets to the female with his beak. She plasters the mud along the sides of the entrance. At last, only a tiny slit remains as an opening. The slit is just wide enough for part of the bill to fit through. For the next six to eight weeks, the male feeds his mate through the small opening. Inside, the imprisoned female lays a few eggs. Protected from snakes, monkeys, and other enemies, the eggs hatch. At the same time, the female loses her old feathers and begins to grow new ones. When the time comes for her to leave her shelter, both the male and the female chip away the hardened mud with their bills.

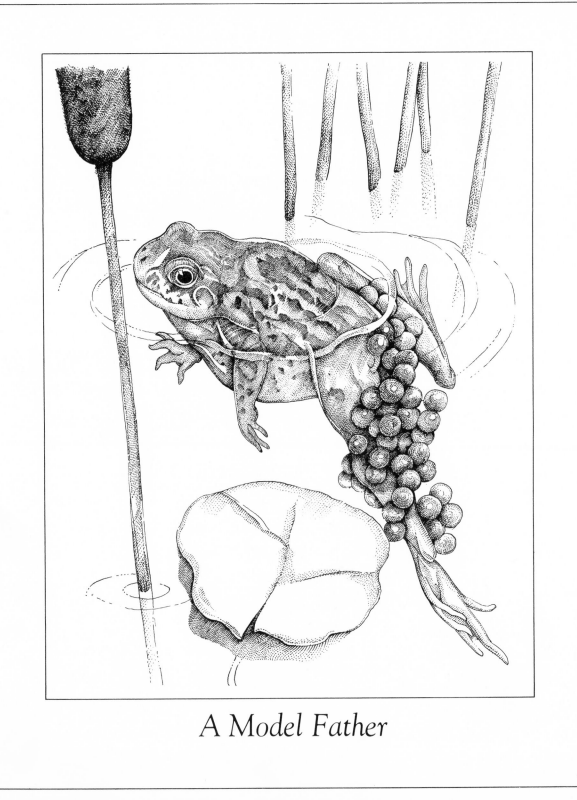

A Model Father

THE MALE MIDWIFE TOAD BECOMES VERY attached to the eggs laid by his mate. In fact, the eggs actually stick to him until they are ready to hatch weeks later! The female toad lays two long strings of eggs, with several dozen in each string. The male fertilizes them and then pushes his legs through the egg mass. The female leaves while the male remains with the eggs stuck to his legs and body. The male then returns to his burrow near a stream or pond. Each of the following nights, the male goes out to feed with the eggs still attached to him. After three weeks, the eggs are about ready to hatch. Within the eggs, the tadpoles are well advanced in their development. They are ready for life on their own. The male carries the eggs to a pond or stream. When the eggs enter the water, the young toads break through the soft coverings. In a few seconds, they are swimming free. They will continue to develop in the pond until they become adult. Then they will leave the water and take up life on the land. The male midwife toad protects the eggs and the young tadpoles from enemies. The eggs and young are safer in the male's burrow than they would be in the waters of a pond or stream.